# DEPARTMENT STORE OF FUTURES

**Lauren Garland** is originally from Leeds. Her poems have appeared in publications including *The London Magazine*, *The North*, *bath magg,* and *Butcher's Dog*. Lauren's debut pamphlet, *Darling*, was published by Broken Sleep Books in 2020. She was the recipient of The Poetry Society's 2021 Peggy Poole Award, working with poet-mentor Paul Farley in 2022/2023.

# Also by Lauren Garland

*Darling*                                        (Broken Sleep Books, 2020)

# CONTENTS

ISBN: 978-1-916938-66-3

Cover designed by Aaron Kent

Edited and Typeset by Aaron Kent

Broken Sleep Books Ltd
PO BOX 102
Llandysul
SA44 9BG

# Department Store of Futures

Lauren Garland

Broken Sleep Books

## AUSTRALIA

April we scribbled names on beer mats,
talked about building a playroom in the garden,
kept ourselves close under a blanket of nausea.

It was a lovely April – I'm glad we had it.
There's summer still. The bathroom to clean,
the electric to pay. We think about emigrating.

I drift around the block, counting up the window cats.
I lounge, phone on flight mode, twinned with my dressing gown.
Below Deck: I love you. I love you more than poetry.

## FLIGHT

You board the flight to lose control.
Passport stowed in a bag overhead
you're nothing more than a blip on a map.
The wing dips without your signal.
If you crash before landing
it won't be your fault.
Submitting to the seatbelt sign
you suppress the urge to stand,
piss, eat – a sandwich only
when the flight attendant chooses.

You end up minding somebody's child.
They're clutching an iPad, dropping ducks
into the right coloured buckets.
Whisky breath on the window side,
you tilt your face towards it
and your mind parachutes back to land
while your body courses further to sea,
to nowhere, and night wipes the view.

## THE ONLY UNBROKEN BENCH

The ice-cream van is gone for the night, and the children
with their pockets full of crusts and lettuce.
The ducks have buried their bills in their feathers.
At the doors to The Pike a light is blinking,
a coin in the gutter blinks up – a face
you don't have a name for. You drift
round the newsagents, its avenues of milk and biscuits,
bin bags and wine. You swing on the swing
where the argument happened, pass the chippy,
the chemist, the nail bar, the allotment, the gate
to your heart is in constant use, there's a lorry
parked across it. Why do you always find yourself here
when the girls are asleep in your childhood bed?
The river is sullen, one wooden rowing boat
drugged by a streetlight, not yielding to the current,
not struggling against it. Your parents watch Casualty
in separate rooms. You swam hard and fast and away.
Now you float, lungs filled with night-time,
back towards the flicker of two televisions.

## RED CLOVER, RASPBERRY LEAF, STINGING NETTLE

I wore rose quartz
on a string round my middle.
We prayed to gods – each in turn,
then all of them at once.
We practised deep breathing
until we ran out of breath.
We holidayed in Greece,
gave our bodies to the sun.

You only have to do it once,
they say – whisky, lust,
leave the condom in your wallet.

We observed the holy days each month.
Talked and didn't talk about it.
Tried to be good – you know,
to deserve it. Twice a week I ran,
not too far, not too fast.
I charted the phases of the moon.
I took my bottom half off,
let the instruments conduct their searches.
I browsed the department store of futures.
My pendulum swung between hope and grief.
I sank from view – a submarine.
I poured away the wine,
trusted my life to bitter green things.

I lay back, relaxed, took a needle through my ovaries.
In the lab they lit a spark made of us.
All we have to do is keep the little flame alive
until it's hot enough to burn a hole in our world
and hand in hand we'll step right through it.

## THE NEIGHBOURS ARE ARGUING ABOUT THE STARS

whether it is, or isn't, Orion's Belt.
I'm lying in the total dark in the new house
with the Artex, the serving hatch,
the symmetrical windows we both loved.
A hand on my tummy scanning for a signal.
A hand on my breast pressing for tenderness,
pushing harder into sleep. It's happening again –

I rev its engine, but the day won't start.
I see your shadow on the landing, telling me
it's time now. You lounge on the counter,
I rinse the mugs, you chatter at the sparrows
nesting in our gutters, dipping to the borders,
calling to each other. Coffee on the sofa
with a space between us and you always fill it.
Tell me you're *not* a motor that runs on love.
My body is a taxi – it gets me to the office,
to Asda, to mum's house. I put cat food
in my trolley, pizza in my mouth. I laugh,
answer *hmm* or *no*. All we talk about is you –

your white belly fur, those tiny incisors,
the way you supervise the pigeons,
nose the sparrow yolk crusted on the patio.

**MURDER!**

This morning, as I poached an egg, you swiped a pigeon from the
blue air. I clapped. You dropped it. I bashed it with a mallet twice.
For hours you rolled in the heap of feathers, bloody streak on your
creamy bib. Now you've climbed onto my lap and into my arms,
insisting on being held. I jog you like a baby. I hush you like a baby
boy, my baby with fur between his toes. We're shuffling round
the living room, radio on to drown out the wind, sort of dancing
round the coffee table – I'm going on instinct the way you do.
The books are there, still and beautiful. The amaryllis on the
windowsill is flowering red. Feathers circle the patio. I drag the
curtain with one hand. I'm thinking about changing our names.

# JUNE BALCONY

Are the clouds moving or is it
the planet spinning? And how fast
the cars go when there are hardly
any of them. But really, I don't
want to think about all that
machinery and the way it works,
the clouds are prodigious today –
so un-Junelike in colour and heft.
Who cares where they came from,
just look at them parading
over the car park and snagged
at the top of the half-clad
apartment block. And next to me
a deck chair – audaciously, classically
blue-white striped – remember
the hip flask on Scarborough beach?
But oh it's sad, the canvas slack
and what's the point of sitting here
naming this pageant of shades
and crowning a winner without you,
it's grey grey blah as supermarket gin.

And the woman on the phone
she's laughing with someone.
She's talking and walking
her labradoodle puppy,
walking and ignoring her puppy
with its teddy bear legs

and ruffle-me curls.
There is so much to be sniffed at
and pissed on and wanted –
the cracks in the pavement
the dirt in the cracks
the abandoned flip flop to worship
from heel to toe and back again.
The rain is back. And if we don't
speak again I hope you're living life
like a labradoodle and lapping
your own face from every puddle.

## TELEPHONE
### After *Summer Afternoon* by Jane Freilicher

Nothing special about the landscape
except that you know it –
perched on your stool, back to the view,
you can plant each tree that flanks the river.
The telephone's fixed to the lilac wall
and you're fixed to your stool, sipping your juice.
You, too, could have a good afternoon –
abandon the glass to the wooden stool,
take a flask to the banks and a book
to doze under. Go ahead, close your eyes,
let the river take your weight.

                      The telephone's ring
will ripple through the juice – the phone
talking to the glass, the glass answering back,
happy, for once, to have the house to themselves.

## LIVING ON THE FLIGHT PATH

4am    the neighbours    asleep

                just the moon    gaping

at the window    a silvery hand on my chest

      the bookcase

         the bed I don't own

                    the moon

         its stethoscope coldness

              and do I have a heartbeat?


     A face should come to mind at night

               it's you again

        or the memory of you

and me    living on the flight path

        nursing Cup a Soups

        and tracing pattern pieces

            under all that noise


     and it's so quiet now in the bedroom

        in the kitchen I'm making a commotion

             in the cutlery draw

        and the wind has nothing to do

        but wrestle itself


somewhere there's a ghost

        with embroidered edges

      and a sidelong smile    I'd like to talk

        to her in passing and

     without words

                    the way the clouds
            converse with the moon


                    and I'd like to sit
                    watch the sun lift
        over the terminal car park
                cars still sleeping
                                        finding
                    their form.

## STILL LIFE

There are thousands
of varieties of apple
to consider.

You stand like a vase
anxious to be filled
with an armful of roses.

The vanity mirror
unveils the answer –
unbearably, it's you.

Grapes slouch over grapes.
The point of the knife
addresses you directly.

A fly makes a fuss
about the mackerel
and it should.

You hover by the easel,
no colour on your brush
but you focus on the fly.

The orange becomes
an orange as you
pick it up and peel it.

## ARCHIPELAGO

Moped propped against the whitewashed wall of a cliffside house.
Paint pots, buckets, pieces of chair. Sea-blue tarpaulin
thrown over a wheelbarrow. Veil of salt thrown over everything.

You sleep through take-off.
I'm half-awake, flicking through a spinner of postcards.
I pull out the one with the junk and the moped, head propped
against the sky, sky thrown over the sea, sea tarpaulin-blue
and thrown over everything.

Somebody rides a sun-busted moped
in the heat of day, spends an hour at the house, rummages in the clutter
for a favourite brush. They scuff the wall as they varnish a door.
They'll fix it tomorrow – a few dabs of white. The task list loops back
and back on itself. It'll take them forever if I want it to.

## ROOMS BY THE SEA
*After Edward Hopper*

A room, its door held open
to the ocean and nothing in this room
but sun – sun accenting the cloud-
brushed wallpaper. I visit the room
at the end of each day and it's always
the same – the way the sea hesitates,
curbs its habit of rushing any cavity,
lingers at the doorway
like an early dinner guest.

I think about leaving my life behind,
finding the room, becoming its minder.
I'd sway on the doorstep
skinny as a heron, testing
my weight against the wind.
I'd plunge into the blue
then haul the catch of my body back up,
ocean dripping from my fingertips.
I'd sleep on the red settee in the back,
take breakfast on the step, the clutter
of my living muddying the palette
of sun against wall, water, room.

## HOLIDAY

Lightning starts, jolting the sky into a new day
that lasts a second. Thunder barks at the whitewashed cottage,

the collie barks back. Moonlight throws itself into the river,
the river tries to carry it away but the moon is fixed

in its position. Lying in bed with the curtains open
you ask them to stop. You ask, won't you please all stop.

# NORTH ATLANTIC SOLO

Knocked along   wave
to wave   the carbon hull
harboured in the arms of
waves   ruined rudder
bow without direction   boat
rocking sleepy   heaving a dream
of salt spray   lighter now
carrying nothing but seafoam
an empty bottle   one oar
lost   one outstretched
waving at the storm clouds
the gulls   the horizon
waving at the waves
and the waves
and the waves

## EMERGENCY EXIT

You walk out the door
and the latch clicks.
Light from the room
bleeds under the door.
You rattle the handle,
try to remember
the source of the light,
its shape, its shade
but the memory blows.

You take the night
by its corners and shake
out the creases, lay it
on the drive, crushing stars
into gravel as you walk
away. A new life flares
somewhere in the distance.
You can't see it yet
but you sense its palpitations.
You put away your map
and haul yourself towards it.

## AFTER THE INCIDENT

A week has passed and I find myself driving,
the wheel trembling under my hands.
It happened hundreds of junctions ago.
I ripped out the mirror so I won't look back.

I turn on the radio. The memory surges
from every station. I feel something growing
where the bitterness was. I'd break squares off my day,
let them melt on your tongue. I mopped up the crumbs

of that yellow apartment. I hope you're there
at the window, jacket zipped all the way up
to your chin and over it, darling. I've only been slowing
for foxes and deer. And I won't slow for you.

## WARNING DO NOT FEED THE HORSES

says the sign, but the horses say they'd like to be fed.
I've lived a bricked-in life with concrete panoramas
knowing nothing about horses – about feeding,
mucking out, their philosophy of haylage and apple.
They tuck their needs under their forelocks.
When did the horses become what I need?
My daily horses, their daily performances –
the dappled one balancing a blackbird on its croup.
The tallest two together, smitten with a tree stump.
The chestnut mare (she has the silkiest ears),
chin on a fencepost, side-eyeing the golf course.

I'm talking about THE HORSES but each is individual
as the residents of a cul-de-sac. At night I lie awake,
the horses wading through my waterlogged mind,
then I dream I'm the mare thundering across the fairway.
Each morning I'm hypnotised by their enigmatic stances.
I find myself guessing what the horses are thinking.
They're thinking is a stable that has no stall for me.

## SHADOW SONNET

In lampless rooms and on moonless nights
we stand dead still, pray for morning.
Our shadows decide how we raise our children.
Our shadows vote in general elections.
The Prime Minister's shadow stands
at the despatch box while the shadow
Shadow Chancellor demands an explanation.
My shadow is heartless –
the way it leads me to the street,
makes me slow dance for the neighbours.
And it really can dance, swelling and shrinking,
shifting its form. Now softer, now sharper.
I'm nothing but an object blocking the light.

## COME OVER

The house is a mess. I'm tired of living
with my finger on my pulse, swaying
to my own pale rhythm. I want to look
in the mirror and see only mirror.
I want to sit like a fruit bowl, ready to be filled
with cantaloupe and lemons. Make me
the window of the abandoned semi –
nothing inside to distract from the alder,
the conifers, the highest of the sycamores.
Suitcases of crockery are cluttering my attic.
Come quickly. Bring bin bags, your music,
your weakness for getting the thing done.

# HOME

The streets are drowsy with fast food
and remembering. The bars have turned
their backs on you and they're walking away.
You hold out your arms without really reaching.
But you're susceptible to this brickwork,
those bus shelters, the bouncer on the corner,
his swaggering refrain. You stray down the alleys
like a lost paramedic, wanting to help
and be helped. The streetlights are yellow or white,
they gather in the rain, guide it into puddles.
You're watching the raindrops falling alone,
forgetting their edges, rippling together.

## ACKNOWLEDGEMENTS

Some of these poems, or earlier versions of them, have appeared in *The London Magazine, The North* and *bath magg.*

Many of the poems in this pamphlet were written during a year's mentorship received as part of the 2021 Peggy Poole Award. Thanks to The Poetry Society for providing this opportunity, and thank you to Paul for the support and encouragement.

Thanks to Aaron Kent and all at Broken Sleep Books for seeing something in these poems.

Love and gratitude to my friends and family, and especially to Francis.

# LAY OUT YOUR UNREST

www.ingramcontent.com/pod-product-compliance
Lightning Source LLC
Chambersburg PA
CBHW051742040426
42447CB00008B/1259